Cheryl Sue

Taylor Franklin

Willie James

Helen Louise

A Cabbage Patch Kids Adventure

Photography by Paul Dube and Mark Gooby

It was a warm, sunny day in the Cabbage Patch, and the 'Kids were sitting around doing absolutely nothing. "I'm bored," said Willy James. "Let's go for an adventure in the woods."

The other Cabbage Patch Kids thought that Willy James' idea was a fine one, and soon they were all off, hiking along a path to the woods.

"We should mark the trails so we don't get lost," said Helen Louise. "Let's tie yellow ribbons to the branches of the trees as we pass. They'll be easy to spot, and they will help us find our way back home."

Once they got into the woods, the 'Kids split up into two groups. The first group charged ahead and had a great time climbing up some steep rocks.

The second group walked through the woods very quietly and discovered a bird's nest with two beautiful eggs in it.

The two groups met at a stream and used the large stones they found there as a path to the other side.

Then it was time for lunch. All the Cabbage Patch
Kids gathered in a meadow near the stream and
unpacked the food they had brought.

After they had eaten as much as their tummies would hold, Evalina Ruth said, "Let's not go yet. Let's sit back and relax. Play us a song on your harmonica, Taylor Franklin, and we'll all sing along."

By the time they had finished singing, Helen Louise
had made a gift for each of them — flower chains
from the beautiful wildflowers she had picked up in
the meadow.

"O.K., everybody get together for a picture," Willy James told the other 'Kids. "I want to have something in my scrap book that will help me remember this day. Come on, smile, Cheryl Sue!"

After the picture taking was over, Tommy George
and Evalina Ruth went fishing...

...while Taylor Franklin got some of the other
Cabbage Patch Kids to help him build a fort.

Later in the afternoon, Helen Louise and Cheryl Sue
picked sides and the 'Kids had a tug of war.

"It's getting late," said Farley Page. "Before we go, let's have a good game of hide and seek. The other 'Kids agreed, and soon they were looking for a hiding place in the woods while Farley Page counted to one hundred.

Willy James and Evalina Ruth hid in a tree. "Shhh!
Stop rustling the branches," whispered Willy James.

Taylor Franklin hid in some bushes, but he soon ran out when he discovered who else was hiding in the bushes.

The sun was setting by the time the Cabbage Patch Kids began to follow the yellow ribbons out of the woods and toward home. "This was a wonderful adventure, Willy James," said Evalina Ruth. "Let's do it again real soon." All the other Cabbage Patch Kids agreed.

Tommy George

Evalina Ruth

Farley Page

*The Day of
Our Adventure*